Looking at Picasso, Altering Cézanne

Peter V. Moak

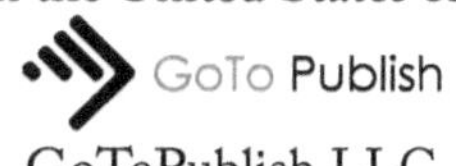

GoToPublish LLC
1-888-337-1724
www.gotopublish.com
info@gotopublish.com

CONTENTS

LOOKING AT PICASSO, ALTERING CÉZANNE

The Visual Ego and the Visual World

The works of Pablo Picasso and Paul Cézanne are based on particular ways of seeing.[1] To understand these ways of seeing I begin with vision. We open our eyes and light passes through the lenses and forms pictures on our retinas. Our brain using these tiny reversed inverted images presents us with a life sized three dimensional stable upright lens projected picture, our *visual world*. We exist and act in relation to our visual world and although it is a picture in our head we see it, as we should, as the external real world. Depth in our interior visual world is represented by diminishing scale which means our visual world is a lens projected picture, a picture of something else, another world, the real outside world. How could it be anything else? I call seeing our interior visual world *vision* and the production of retinal pictures *eyesight*. We see our interior visual world in two basic ways. The first I call *nonaligned* and the second *aligned*. We see our unaligned visual world as separate from us and not around us. Although upright, reversed and apparently much enlarged our nonaligned visual world is similar to a lens projected retinal picture. My eyes as the center of my being stand outside the nonaligned visual world and not in it. When I physically move including just my eyes I extend my nonaligned visual world but I do not enter it. I enter my visual world when I become aligned. I do this by imagining a point in the visual world lined up with an imagined point behind my eyes, my *point of view.* These points come into being when I imagine them together with a *line of sight* stretching between them. I call my aligned presence in relation to the visual world, my eyes together with my point of view, my *visual ego* which is now the center of my aligned visual world and the center of my being.[2] When surrounding points in the visual world are seen aligned with my point of view lines and objects in the visual world appear standing still and regularized in a way I can remember them, visualize them and relate them to each other. Changing eye size is called widening or narrowing of the eyes even though we can not physically change the size of our eyes. However I can seem to do so by imagining points at the corners of my eyes aligned with my point of view and changing the distance between these points. I can move in and out in my visual by holding a point if the visual world still at the same time moving my point of view back from or toward it. This is one way I separate adjacent objects in depth. I call this *scale reduction.* If I make the apparent size of our eyes smaller than an object I move close to the object and the outlines of the object are spread out around me. A small close up visual ego can make a distant object appear life sized a phenomena called *constancy scaling.* If I make my visual ego larger than an object the object is seen across space and spread out in front of me. When I move spacial continuity between objects is maintained if before I move I become peripherally aligned to the next object. If I do not do this the next object is seen in a separate space and what I call *disconnected.* Using the above elements of my vision: nonalignment, alignment, the visual ego, moving and changing the size of the visual ego, perspective, point of view, lines of sight, peripheral alignment, regularized outlines, memorable shapes, spacial continuity, disconnection and constancy scaling I geometrically order my relationship to my visual world. This relationship places me at the center of my visual world in ways that compensate for the separateness and diminishing scale of the lens projected nonaligned visual world turning it into a world that more closely resembles the outside physical world. Another ability that influences the way I see is the power to keep up to four things in my mind at once.

The memorable visual units created by the geometric ordering of vision together with the ability to hold one to four units in my mind at the same time enhances my ability to make works of art. The counter intuitive way I describe vision sounds strange. We are not conscious of the visual procedures, the mental gymnastics I describe. Normal vision seems effortless and automatic. For example we adjust the size of our eyes when we look at television or at the movies without knowing it. Be that as it may my experience is that being aware of your visual ego and its actions is necessary when it comes to looking at works of art. <u>I find that a *work of art* is a thing made by a human being using an aligned visual ego in a particular way that I call the *perspective.*</u> Thus to see a work of art correctly we need to use the same perspective used when it was made. By perspective I do not mean linear perspective, a mechanical drawing procedure that imitates the linear structure and diminishing scale of a lens projected picture and does not require a particular use of the aligned visual ego. I find the right perspective through trial and error. The right perspective makes a work of art look its *aesthetic best* which I find to be a universal resulting from parts that cohere and not a matter of *taste*, taste being an individual or social preference. I find *style* to be a mix of characteristics, the perspective being just one. I see things made by animals, or the unmodified photograph and as not depending on an aligned visual ego so not as works of art. For this reason I believe the visual ego is unique to modern human beings, Homo sapiens sapiens. We are a species of artists. I see patterns in perspective used in history. I see different perspectives following the peopling of the earth which begins in Africa and spreads from there, the Noah's Ark theory.[3] I also see changes in perspective following the evolution of a culture, for example Greek culture from the tenth through the first century B.C. In Europe along with vast social and political changes from the first century B.C. to the twelfth century A.D. and beyond I find perspectives changing. Beginning in Spain in the eleventh century A.D. I find standard perspectives appearing for the emerging nation-states of the West. In the East perspective use remains relatively constant. In the following centuries the perspective used by individual artists becomes important. Since the second half of the twentieth century there has been an effort to escape the bounds created by perspective, the closed world that is a work of art. I find this effort misguided.

PERSPECTIVES RELEVANT TO THE WORK OF PICASSO AND OF CÉZANNE

(the names are mine)

Semitic perspective The visual ego is smaller than the object. Continuity with the next object is maintained. If you peripherally align the next object with you point of view before you move. If you do not do this the next object is first seen unaligned and disconnected. I find Semitic perspective in the early art of the people speaking the Semitic languages and so the name. Coming to Western Europe from North Africa in the later middle ages it becomes the most widely used perspective in the Western World.

Oriental perspective The visual ego is larger than the object. The large ego is placed back from the object which is spread out before you and is more planar than the Semitic perspective object. To remain continuously aligned when using Oriental perspective you again see following objects peripherally aligned. I find Oriental perspective common to China, Japan, Korea, South East Asia, the art of Central and South America and that of the native American peoples of North America.

Peripheral Perspective In contrast to Semitic and Oriental perspective that place you before an object peripheral perspective places you to the side of an object. Seen in this way the object or a portion thereof is seen obliquely aligned and the composition part by part. I find peripheral perspective to have a long history beginning with the very early art of peoples speaking the Indo-European languages. It is today a characteristic of the art of Indian and Post Modern architecture.

African Perspective begins with a shape seen nonaligned and then seen center aligned with a close by small visual ego. This procedure isolates shapes that confront you in turn. African perspective is a characteristic of art from sub-Saharan Africa and very early works of art coming from a "path" stretching from sub-Saharan Africa across the Mediterranean to India.

European Perspective is basic to the art of Stone Age Europe, Old Europe. European perspective shapes are first seen nonaligned and then side aligned with a small ego. As with African perspective disconnection isolates each shape in turn. European perspective is found in Etruscan and Roman art.

LOOKING AT PICASSO

Pablo Picasso, 1887-1971, is famous for the variety and inventiveness of his art which has been explained by his biography, his influence, philosophy, politics, history and culture, but not by his ways of seeing, his art, his perspectives.[4] I find Picasso using eleven different perspectives during his lifetime which he never explained. To understand them we must look to his work.

Picasso's First Perspective.

Picasso was born in Malaga, Spain on October 25th, 1881 His father, Jose Ruiz Blasco was a drawing teacher and painter whose use of wide-view Hellenic perspective gives his works a coherence not found in his son's. In 1891 Picasso's family moved to La Coruna, Spain and in 1895 to Barcelona were Picasso entered art school. In October 1900 Picasso made his first visit to Paris to see the Universal Exposition at which he had a painting, *Science and Charity*, 1900, Picasso Museum, Barcelona and to learn about the Paris art world.[5] The painting is based on Picasso's First perspective a small fixed ego at the bottom center of the composition bottom aligned to reduced scale forms first seen unaligned and then bottom aligned with with small ego. The painting has many pleasing passages, the head of the doctor, a portrait of his father, the child, and because of the fixed bottom ego is coherent.[6] While in Paris Picasso made a painting of a Parisian dance hall, *Le Moulin de la Galette,* 1900, compare this to Toulouse Lautrec's *At the Moulin Rouge, 1892, The Art Institute of Chicago*, a similar subject which is a unified, wide view, Semitic perspective composition filled with curvilinear shapes and harmonious color of Art Nouveau. In the Picasso some of the shapes are curvilinear while others are angular and discordant. This dissonance was perhaps even more disturbing at the time than the lesbians in the foreground. However it is dissonance that energizes this nocturnal scene and sets it apart. Picassos's use of nonalignment is a strength. Picasso came to Paris to catch up. When he Leaves that same year he is already ahead.

Picasso's Second Perspective.

In the fall of 1901 on a second trip to Paris Picasso discovers peripheral perspective. It would seem that the change was inspired by the woodcuts of the French painter Paul Gauguin then in Tahiti that were in the hands of with a mutual friend the Basque sculptor and ceramist Paco Durio.[8] Seen in a Picasso drawing, *Parisian and Exotic Figures*, 1901, Picasso Museum, Paris, are images based on a small peripherally aligned ego with forms first seen unaligned. The drawing of the the figure to the left suggest such Gauguin woodcuts as *Te Atua,* 1892, Art Institute Chicago, which is based on a wide-view peripheral perspective. Paul Gauguin discovered peripheral perspective at the 1889 Paris Worlds Fair.[9] Because he discovered peripheral perspective in art from India and Indonesia he may have thought it non western. Ironically it is a characteristic of the early art of the Indo-European speaking peoples. Gauguin's *Portrait of a Woman with a Still Life By Cézanne,* 1890, Art Institute of Chicago, indicates that this was a conscious change in perspective.[10] The woman in the chair is based on peripheral perspective while the Cézanne still life on the wall is based on Gauguin's original center aligned Semitic perspective. The real Cézanne which Gauguin owned at the time is based on Cézanne perspective which begins with wide-view Oriental perspective. In this context individual forms are seen as nonaligned and so disconnected and then seen individually center aligned with a large ego. At times Gauguin switches back to Semitic perspective which is similar to Picasso's alternating perspectives. Gauguin deserves credit for inspiring a major turning point that will effect Picasso's entire career. Picasso like Gauguin documented his change in perspective with a painting, the *Blue Room*, 1901, Philips Collection, Washington D.C.[11] The area above the bed including a Lautrec poster is based on Semitic perspective while the bathing girl and her surroundings are based on his Second perspective, peripheral perspective.. With his blue period Barcelona painting *The Blind Man's Meal*, 1903, Metropolitan Museum of Art, New York City, Picasso gives us a reason for his use of peripheral perspective. Seen here is a blind street singer seated at a table holding a piece of bread and touching a jug. As the obliquely presented forms sequentially materialize they seem touchable giving blindness and poverty a physical presence.[12] The illusion of a tactile presence will be a major concern of Picasso. Picasso used peripheral perspective for five years, his so called Blue and Rose periods.

Picasso's Third Perspective.

In the fall of 1906 after a summer in Spain Picasso adopts this Third perspective.

A large peripherally aligned ego with forms first seen unaligned which is the same as Two except the ego is now large. Picasso sees forms peripherally from his Blue period on. A work that marks the change in perspective is *Peasants and Oxen*, fall 1906, Barnes Foundation, Philadelphia.[13] Disconnection allows for the startling inconsistencies in color and scale between shapes. See Picasso's *Two Nudes*, 1906, Museum of Modern Art, New York City, where two full length, hulking female nudes face each other before a brown curtain.[14] There is a suggestion of a mirror images, but they are strangely different. Even stranger is the relationship between their parts. Disconnected parts permits the radical differences in scale, color and point of view.

For example the head of the figure on our left is smaller in scale than her torso while her hand and arm are larger still. Picasso gives these images a presence, a new "reality", by the change in character as we move around the figures. The radically disconnected shapes are another a major step toward what is to come. This change in perspective may have been motivated by two portraits in the collection of Leo and Gertrude Stein. These are Cézanne's *Portrait of the Artists Wife*, before 1885, Foundation Brülrle, Zurich and Matisse's *Woman with a Hat*, 1905, San Francisco Museum of Art.[15] The Cézanne is based on Cézanne perspective and the Matisse on a perspective Matisse adopts in 1905, the composition as a whole based on wide view with individual forms seen nonaligned and individually aligned with a the large ego.[16] It would seem that the radical nature of these portraits was apparent to Picasso, but maybe not their perspectives. In the spring of 1906 using peripheral perspective Picasso began painting his *Portrait of Gertrude Stein, 1906*, Metropolitan Museum of Art, New York City.15 After many sittings he leaves this unfinished only to take it up again in the fall of 1906 when he repaints only the face using his Perspective Three. The disconnection of the face and figure anticipates Picasso's use of systematic incongruities in works to come.

Picasso's Fourth Perspective.

In late 1906 and early 1907 Picasso began making studies for a large painting, the future *Les Demoiselles d'Avignon*, 1907-8, Museum of Modern Art, New York City. When I arrange the drawings in accordance with the number of figures, the poses and the perspective at a certain point a strange female figure with a triangular torso and arms that form a rectangle around her head appears which is similar to mourning figures found on Attic protogeometric vases.[17] At first this figure is based on Picasso's Third perspective. But a large drawing of the figure, *Figure Seen From the Back*, 1907, Picasso Museum, Paris, has its outlines changed except for those of the head so that it is now based on Picasso's Fourth perspective,[18] With the Fourth perspective a large ego located on the picture plane. is peripherally aligned to forms first seen unaligned, The flatten shapes are cut out by dark lines and areas. As a result images appear composed of cut out, disconnected, flattened, startlingly immediate shapes. An inspiration for this new perceptive may have been the work of Cézanne and Matisse, but I think a more likely source is the protogeometric Greek vase painting where I think Picasso found the figure with rectangular arms. These vase paintings are based on African perspective, a small ego center aligned to shapes first seen unaligned, a survivor from the Mycenaean era. Having found his perspective Four Picasso proceeds to paint *Les Demoiselles d'Avignon*. Because he later repaints the right and left sides of the picture with a Fifth and Sixth perspective. The painting is today a three part picture. Only the center part including a standing and a seated figure and a gray background curtain are based on perspective Four.

Picasso's Fifth Perspective.

Shortly after completing his first version of *Les Demoiselles* Picasso using perspective Four Picasso modified Four by using an initially small ego. With the Fifth perspective a small ego located on the picture plane. is peripherally aligned to forms first seen unaligned, The perspective Five shapes are even more immediate than perspective Four shapes. Some Picasso drawings based on perspective Five in an April 1907 catalogue of a Daumier exhibition suggest Oceanic art may have inspired perspective five even though Oceanic perspective is based on a large ego.[19] A drawing in this catalogue of a frontal female nude with hands clasped below her waist along with a painting, *Woman with Joined Hands*, 1907, Picasso Museum, Paris are based on perspective Fve. The pose and form of this figure suggest the *Female New Caledonian Roof Finial*, Picasso Museum Paris, that Picasso owned.[20] The water color, *Five Nudes*, 1907, Philadelphia Museum of Art which is based on perspective Five shows that Picasso considered repainting the entire *Les Demoiselles d'Avignon* using perspective Five.[21] Around this time Picasso visited the Trocodéro Museum and is struck by the power of African and Oceanic art to "mediate with the world of the spirits."[22] He may have seen African and Oceanic shapes as similar to those in his own new work and that his new perspective gave him similar powers. The influence of African and Oceanic art is clearly seen in the pronounced shapes, striping, strong colors and disparate scaling of the heads of the two figures on the right whose mask like faces seem made from pieces of wood. Today only the right side of the painting, the standing and the squatting figure, the blue curtain and the still life on a table are based on perspective Five.

Picasso's Sixth Perspective.

In early 1908 Picasso uses perspective Six to repaint the woman pushing back a brown curtain on the left. With Six a small ego aligned to point beyond the picture is peripherally aligned to shapes first seen unaligned producing more robust forms that Five..[23] At this time Picasso completes *Les Demoiselles d'Avignon* using perspective Six by repainting the figure on the left who strides onto the scene while brushing back a brown curtain. Today *Les Demoiselles d'Avignon* stands out because of its radical appearance and its parade of three new perspectives. I find that all five "Demoiselles" including the mask like faces on the right correctly seen have the face of Picasso's companion Fernand Olivier laying to rest the idea that the painting is about sex or disease or that it denigrates women. For me the five monumental women rise up to celebrate womanhood and the beautiful Fernand.

Picasso's Perspective Seven.

During the summer of 1908 while working north of Paris at La Rue des Bois Picasso again varies his perspective. Perspective Seven is like Six except the ego is large. With Seven a large ego aligned to a point beyond the picture is peripherally aligned to shapes first seen unaligned.[23] See *Landscape, La Rue des Bois*, 1906, Museum of Modern Art, New York City.[24] Picasso will use perspective Seven until the fall of 1909. In the fall of 1908 he completes the large three figure composition, *Three Women*, 1907-8, Hermitage Museum, St. Petersburg, which begins as a perspective Five work, is repainted using perspective Six and finally again repainted using perspective Seven.[25] Seen here are three robust women who despite their heft are entirely feminine.[26] The experience is moving before a monumental sculpture in relief in contrast to the more planar *Les Demoiselles d'Avignon*. In early 1908 while working on *Three Women* Picasso is visited by Georges Braque. Braque's original perspective is Oriental perspective with a narrow large ego. Sometime after meeting Picasso and seeing *Three Women* Braque begins seeing forms nonaligned before they are seen aligned with a large ego. See Braque's *Large Nude*, 1908, Private Collection.[27] In the fall of 1908 Braque begins exhibiting "Picasso-like" works which come to be called Cubism. Soon two other French artists, Fernand Léger and Robert Delauney and a little later the Catalan, Juan Gris begin seeing forms nonaligned before seeing them aligned to the small ego. From here Cubism spreads around the world.[28]

Picasso's Perspective Eight.

Picasso spends the summer of 1909 at Horta de San Juan, Spain where he paints perspective Seven works including *Reservoir*, 1909, Private Collection, a view across an animal watering pool to houses on a hill top where the viewer jumps goat like from house to house.[29] In the fall of 1909 Picasso returns to Paris where he introduces perspective Eight. With Eight a small ego located beyond the picture is peripherally aligned to surfaces originally seen unaligned. See *Still Life with a Liqueur Bottle*, 1909. Museum of Modern Art, New York City painted at Horta Spain using perspective Seven and repainted in Paris, fall 1909 using perspective Eight.[30] The composition centers on a ceramic rooster, a vessel for drinking wine around which beginning in the upper right are a distant mountain, a folded newspaper, a glass, a liqueur bottle lying on its side and another bottle standing in the lower left. Behind the table are the folds of a green curtain. During the winter of 1909-10 Picasso's pictures become more and more puzzles to be solved. The perspective Eight, *Girl with a Mandolin*, 1909-10, Museum of Modern Art, New York City, shows a half-length female nude posed before stacked canvases in the artist's studio.[31] The rounded contours of her easily recognizable breasts and those of the mandolin stand in contrast to the rectangular shapes that make up her face. Degree of legibility is the artist's option.

Picasso's Perspective Nine.

In the fall of 1910 Picasso repainted several paintings from a summer at Cadaques Spain using his perspective Nine. With Nine a large ego aligned to a point beyond the picture is peripherally aligned to open surfaces with unaligned divisions in contrast to images made up of closed shapes as with perspective Eight. See *Guitarist*, summer 1910, repainted fall 1910, National Museum of Modern Art, Paris.[32] Follow the open disconnected shapes and a half length figure of a singing man holding a mandolin emerges (guitar is a misnomer). His left arm supports the neck of the instrument while his right hand supports its base. Notice how dark along edges cuts out shapes. Only slightly less enigmatic is the precisely painted *Portrait of Daniel Henry Kahnweiler*, winter of 1910-11, The Art Institute of Chicago.[33] Picasso has framed this perspective Nine, half length seated portrait of his dealer with a collection of African and Oceanic works of art. In addition to describing such works as magical Picasso called them rational.[34] Kahnweiler's mask like face spread across rectangular facets may be an amusing reference to the reason Kahnweiler sought in Picasso's cubism. Another Variation Six work that is almost a pendant to the *Kahnweiler Portrait* is *Portrait of a Woman*, 1910, Museum of Fine Arts, Boston which seems to embody the magical side of African and Oceanic art.[35] Follow the bouncing facets and you find a half length female nude seated in a chair who's left hand holds an "African"mask above her shrouded in shadow face. Around her float a group of African and Oceanic works of art. Their flickering presence is reminiscent of the Gauguin woodcuts that first put Picasso on the road to cubism. Picasso spent the summer of 1911 at Céret in the South of France. He uses Perspective Nine to paint a number of figure compositions, still lives and a landscape in which are Picasso and his pet monkey. See

Landscape by Céret, 1911, Guggenheim Museum, New York. From the following winter comes *Ma Jolie, Woman with a Zither*, 1911, Museum of Modern Art, New York City.[36] This Variation Nine painting of a half length seated nude woman holding a zither includes a portrait of Eva Gouel and a secret portrait of Picasso. Seeing the composition step by step reveals the nude Eva holding a zither in the crook of her right arm while her left hand rests on the strings of the Zither. Surrounding her beginning in the upper right are a curtain, a bit of decorative cord, a large tassel, an arm of her chair, a sheet of music with the words "Ma Jolie" (the name of a popular song), the other arm of the chair, a glass on a table, the head of a cat and what may look like a still life is actually the very geometric face of Picasso, pipe in mouth, perhaps caught in a mirror.[37]

Perspective Ten.

Sometime in the spring of 1912 Picasso adopts perspective Ten. With Ten a small ego aligned to a point on the picture surface is peripherally aligned to open surfaces with unaligned.divisions. At this time Picasso begins using collage a natural adjunct to works composed of surfaces seemingly cut from the picture surface. See *Still Life with Chair Canning*. 1912, Picasso Museum, Paris.[38] Seen here are a newspaper, pipe, glass, knife, slice of lemon and scollop shell on a table next to a caned chair seat. To the painting Picasso has added a piece of oil cloth printed to look like chair caning and a piece of rope as a frame. The trick, the illusion, is in the perspective context these additions look as painted as everything else.

Perspective Eleven.

Picasso will use Ten through the summer of 1912. That fall he repaints some of his summer 1912 pictures using perspective Eleven. With Eleven a large ego aligned to points on the on the picture plane is peripherally aligned to open surfaces with divisions seen unaligned.

Eleven is the same as Ten except for the large ego. See *Man with a Hat*, a self portrait drawing with collage and painted elements, 1912, Museum of Modern Art, New York City. *Man with a Guitar*, 1912, Philadelphia Museum of Art is one of the summer 1912 perspective Ten paintings Picasso repainted in the fall of 1912 using perspective Eleven.[39] Shown here is a man dressed as a bullfighter holding a guitar and seated at a table on which rests some sort of conical confection. That fall Picasso begins making pasted paper compositions using perspective Eleven. These line drawings that in some cases include painted shapes and pieces of newspaper, ephemera made permanent. With *Man with a Hat*, 1912, Museum of Modern Art, New York City, a self portrait, the piece of newspaper sets off a shape and suggests shadow.[40] That fall Picasso makes a perspective Eleven cardboard sculpture, *Guitar*, 1912, Museum of Modern Art, New York. Picasso says the idea for representing the sound hole of the guitar as a cylinder which places it on a different plane came from a *Grebo Mask* which he owned, Picasso Museum, Paris,. Nevertheless the effect of the *Mask* and the Guitar is quite different. The not aligned forms of the mask mysteriously materialize in a manner consistent with its religious nature.

I see the Guitar as an everyday object the parts of which materializing and then fading away as if in a dream or memory, a past recaptured.[41] Picasso's sculpture being based on the same basic perspectives reside in the same fractured illusionary space as his paintings and drawings.

And Beyond

Picasso continues to use Eleven until the spring of 1914 when he returns to Ten, see *Pipe Glass and Bottle of Rum*, Museum of Modern Art, New York City.[42] Picasso's practice is to use Ten or Eleven for a period of time and then switch to the other. From time to time Picasso use close shapes peripheral perspective, See perspective Two *Portrait of of Max Jaco*, 1915 private collections and perspective Three *Tree Woman at a Spring*, 1921, Museum Of Modern Art, New York In December 1915 Picasso writes Gertrude Stein about visits to a clinic where Eva is dying and about a recent work, *Harlequin*, 1915, Museum of Modern Art, New York City.[43] This Variation ten *Harlequin* pictures Harlequin the trickster, Picasso's sometime alter ego, leaning on a table holding a portrait of Picasso.[44] Concealed in the scumbling that picks out Picasso's profile is the barely discernible emaciated face of Eva.[45] Much has been made of the relationship between Picasso's private life and his art and rightfully so as Picasso's private life is often the subject in his work. However it does not mean that knowing about his private life tells us how to look at his work which we need to properly connect his life and work. His perspective Ten, *Nude Woman, "Jaime Eva"*, 1912, Columbus Museum of Art, Columbus, Ohio, depicts a standing, largely nude Eva holding a card saying "Jaime Eva."[46] Draped around her I see the previously not identified Picasso whose hands frame her breasts. What seems a less affectionate view of Eva is found in Picasso's perspective Ten collage *Au Bon Marché*, 1912-13, Ludwig Collection, Aachen, Germany. Here a box top from a Paris department store, an advertisement from another Paris store which refers to feminine apparel and some wall paper make up a cash register toward which a hand gestures. Picasso's? On the right in the guise of a glass are the head and shoulders of a woman whose downcast eyes suggest shame while on the left is the head of Picasso's faithful dog Frika in the guise of a bottle [47] Another "still life" where Picasso's private life is present in the disguise of a perspective Ten still life. *Still Life with a Pedestal Table*, 1931, Picasso Museum, Paris. Posing as a compote on a table is the dancing Marie-Térese Walter, Picasso's young mistress who lifts her skirts to her waste. On her right is a huge head with rolling eye. Stranger still, caught in the handle of a yellow pitcher is a head wearing a crown like that worn by Herrod in Picasso's 1905 dry point, *Salomé*. It would seem that Marie-Térese is Salomé and the head of St. John the Baptist, Picasso.[48] In 1948 we find Picasso again playing games under the cover of his peculiar perspective with two paintings titled *The Kitchen*, 1948, Picasso Museum, Paris and Museum of Modern Art, New York City. Francoise Gilot, Picasso's companion and mother of two of his children writes that under Picasso's direction she began the second, the New York, by producing a minimal version of the first which Picasso had complicated with "real details," plates, bird cadges and a potted plant. Both these perspective Ten compositions turn out to contain two large heads, baby Claude' on the right and Francoise kissing baby Claude on the cheek. In the upper left is the face of Picasso/[49]

Following Ten Picasso uses perspective Eleven for a little over a year, fall 1915 to early 1917, when, in Rome he returns to Ten. He continues to use Ten until the summer of 1921 when at Fontainebleau he paints to two large cubist canvases called The *Three Musicians*. The first is based on perspective Ten, Museum of Modern Art, New York City and the second on Eleven, the Philadelphia Museum of Art. A third, large painting from Fontainebleau, *Three Women*, 1921, Museum of Modern Art, New York City is based on perspective Three.[50] In the fall of 1923 Picasso returns to perspective Ten which he uses until the fall of 1935. From the fall of 1935 through the summer of 1941 he uses Eleven. He will then use Ten till 1965 when he turns to Eleven which he will use until his death in 1973. One occasion where he uses more than one perspective for the same work is *Girl Before a Mirror*, 1932, The Museum of Modern Art, New York City. The perspective Ten pregnant Marie Terrase pops out at us while her perspective Eleven image in the mirror floats mysteriously away.[51]

Understanding Picasso's perspectives provides us an entry into his art and also a tool for better understating the whole history of art and in particular the work of his great progenitor, Paul Cézanne to which we now turn.

ALTERING CÉZANNE

Cézanne's Perspective

When I compare Paul Cézanne's *Large Bathers*, R856, The Barnes Foundation, Philadelphia, to Emile Bernard's 1904 photograph of Cézanne seated before this painting I come to a disturbing conclusion. The Barnes *Large Bathers* appears to not entirely based on Cézanne's perspective while the painting in the photograph is entirely a Cézanne. Previously I had suspected a number of Cézanne's paintings of not being by Cézanne, but the Barnes *Bathers* was certainly a Cézanne. So this was something else, a Cézanne being altered, mostly in its outlines using a perspective not used by Cézanne. Cézanne's perspective as I see it, his way of seeing and composing his works, begins with a center aligned large ego producing a wide view of the composition. In this context individual reduced scale shapes are first seen nonaligned and disconnected and then individually aligned to the large ego. In this way Cézanne individualizes his shapes in a composition that is held together by a wide view. In addition Cézanne forms are seen center aligned and diminished in scale. A Cézanne composition is a sequence of disconnected and then aligned shapes shapes bound together by an overall view (around 1885 Cézanne begins fixing the position of his ego).

Altering

Perspective structures a work of art, gives it coherence. Changing a work using a perspective not used in it its creation diminishes it I see outlines changed using Semitic perspective in at least 90 Cézanne paintings in the Rewald catalogue.[52] Others including the Barnes *Bathers* R856, I find more completely repainted using Semitic perspective. How did this happen? Did Cézanne, aging and diabetic, after many years defending his individuality against harsh criticism begin altering his paintings with a different perspective all the while continuing to produce masterpieces using his original perspective?[53] If not Cézanne then who? It might have been at the direction Ambroise Vollard, Cézanne's dealer, who along with Cézanne's son Paul seems to have had the necessary access for 93 paintings in the Rewald catalogue to be altered.[54] In addition to Vollard I find seven others, all artists, altering Cézannes in their possession. These are: Camille Pissaro, four; Edgar Degas, six; Claude Monet, two; Emile Schuffenecker, two; Egisto Fabbri, twelve; Henri Matisse, four and Pablo Picasso two.[55]

1859-1872

Cézanne was born in 1839. In the Rewald catalogue paintings date from as early as 1859. From this date to the spring of 1872 when he went to work with Pissaro I find three significant works as altered. The first is R121, *The Abduction*, 1867, on loan to the Fitzwilliam Museum, Cambridge. Here I see the contours of the struggling central figures, a man and a woman, redrawn using Semitic perspective which leaves them an anatomical jumble. Another early loss is R136, *The Black Clock*, 1867-1869, Private Collection, long regarded a Cézanne masterpiece. Could it be that it reputation rests on is refashioned conventual Semitic perspective outlines? A third early loss is R149, *Young Girl at the Piano, Overture to Tannheuser*, 1869-70, Hermitage Museum, St. Petersburg in which Cézanne placed his sisters in what would have been an intricately balanced domestic interior. I see reworked Semitic perspective outlines comprising both figures and furniture. Only the wallpaper and fabric on a chair look to me intact. In addition to these three early losses, owed I suspect to Vollard, we have R120, *The Negro Scipion*, 1867, Museo de Arte Sao Paulo, Assis Chateaubriand, which once belonged to Claude Monet and which on the basis on a fixed ego Attic perspective I suspect as heavily repainted by Monet.[56] Finally we have two well known works from the end of the early years which I believe misattributed. These are R179, *The Wine Depot*, 1872, Private Collection and R182, *Portrait of Cézanne*, 1872, Musée d'Orsay. These I see as based on the Hellenic perspective used by Cézanne's friend the painter Achille Emperaire.[57]

1872-82

From the "Pissaro decade", 1872-82, come ten more paintings I believe altered at the behest of Vollard, R201, R280, R291, R293, R299, R305, R407, R428, R452 and R464. I also find three I think altered by Camille Pissaro, R302, R313 and R385; three by Edgar Degas, R346, R369 and R416; six by Egisto Fabbri, R124, R324, R341, R425, R429 and R438; one by Henri Matisse, R360 and two by Pablo Picasso, R365 and R395. I also find R188 not to be by Cézanne but by Paul Renoire. I find one of the losses to Vollard is R201, *The House of Pierre Lacroix*, 1872, National Gallery of Art, Washington, DC. This work from Cézanne's first summer with Pissaro was shown at the First Impressionist Exhibition, 1879. What remains today is for me only a suggestion of what once was. Look to R220, *Houses at Auvers*, c.1873, Fogg Museum, Cambridge, MA, to see how early on Cézanne eclipsed impressionism by the inventiveness of his brushwork, forms and color. From the end of the Pissaro years comes R407, *Poplars*, 1879-80, Musée d'Orsay, I think this is another loss probably to Vollard and Semitic perspective outlines. As originally conceived it would have anticipated Cézanne of the eighties and nineties, the "classical" Cézanne ("classical" in the sense that Cézanne's compositions from this time appear more harmonious and geometric). Compare *Poplars* to, *The Bridge at Mainecy*, R436, 1879-80, Musée d'Orsay, where Cézanne's unique geometry prevails in all it strength and subtlety. Three Cézannes from the seventies I believe altered by Pissaro who once owned them and because I see now largely based on the fixed ego Semtic perspective used by Pissaro. These are *Still Life with a Soup Tureen*, R302, ca 1877, Musée d'Orsay, *Two Vases of Flowers*, R313, 1877, private collection and *Portrait of Paul Cézanne*, R383, 1877, Musée d'Orsay.[58] I believe Edgar Degas, on the basis of the Hellenic perspective he used and his one time ownership to be responsible for reworking R346, *Seven Apples*, ca 1878, Keynes Collection, on loan to the Fitzwilliam Museum, Cambridge; *Bather with Raised Arms*, R369, 1874-80, Private Collection and *Portrait of Cézanne*, R416, 1879-80, Private Collection.[59] John Rewald suggests that the frequently reproduced, *Panoramic View of Auvers*, R221, 1873-4, Chicago Art Institute, once belonged to the Cézanne supporter Dr. Paul Gachet. I see this as a Semitic perspective composition of dubious merit and not a Cézanne. It could well be by one of the Gachets, father or son.[60] I see four Cézanne paintings from this period presumably repainted by the Italian American amateur painter and early Cézanne collector, Egisto Fabbri, their one time owner. Of the four, I think our greatest loss is *Madame Cézanne in a Striped Skirt*, R324, 1877, The Museum of Fine Arts, Boston which I see as quixotically repainted using Semitic perspective. Left untouched are the wall paper, the right side of her red armchair and her skirt. Compare this to a true Cézanne, *Madame Cézanne Sewing*, R323, c. 1877, The Nationals Museum of Art, Stockholm, for the beauty of its geometry, now so lacking in what I see as the confused forms of the Boston painting. Another loss to Fabbri is *Houses in Provence*, R438, National Gallery of Art, Washington, DC. I suspect that this well known "Cézanne", much admired for its geometry is now more Fabbri than Cézanne and has done much to obscure the real Cézanne. Sadly find such important losses to Fabbri continue with "Cézannes from the eighties.[61]

A most distressing and confusing case is that of the *Three Bathers*, R360, 1876-77, Musée de la Ville de Paris, Petite Palais. This famous "Cézanne" was given to the City of Paris in 1936 by Henri Matisse, who said it had inspired him. Be that as it may, I see it as heavily repainted using a Matisse's perspective and no longer as a Cézanne,[62]

Just as disturbing is the case of two "Cézannes" in the Picasso Museum Paris, R365, *Five Bathers*, 1877-78 and R395, *l'Estaque Seen Through Trees*, 1878-79. Both I see as largely repainted Picasso's perspective Ten.[63] Compare Picasso's R365 to R364, a similar, intact, five bather Cézanne composition and R395 to R396, a similar intact Cézanne landscape. These Picasso\Cézannes have merit as Picassos, but I see them as poor things compared to real Cézannes.

1882-95

In the midst of Cézanne's career is the period 1882-95, spent working around Aix. From here come 40 paintings I see as altered probably at the behest of Vollard (see appendix nos. R513 through R804). I also see as altered; two by Pissaro, R455 and R577; one by Degas, R557; one by Monet, R666; one by Matisse, R576; one by Emile Schuffenecker, R537 and four by Egisto Fabbri; R551, R569, R659 and R717. I suspect R530, *l'Estaque, Rocks, Pines and The Sea*, ca 1880, Staatliche Kunsthalle, Karlsruhe to be a loss to Vollard. Compare this to R531, *L'Estaque and The Golf of Marseilles*, ca 1880, on loan to the Fitzwilliam Museum, Cambridge. I see the incongruous outlines imposed on the Karlsruhe painting destroying the dynamic balancing that so distinguishes the intact Cambridge painting . The same contrast I find exists between R626, *The Golf of Marseilles Seen from L'Estaque*, 1885-86, The Art Institute, Chicago and R625, *The Golf of Marseilles Seen From L'Estaque*. The Metropolitan Museum of Art, New York. The New York painting is a beautifully realized, serenely coherent and wonderfully diverse work of art. From the plunge to horizontal roof tops in the lower right to the vertically accented central fore and middle ground buildings to the alternating green and gold headlands on the left that give way to a subtly varied plane of blue water, to the violet solidity of the the hills of the Marseillivegre and finally to an azure sky all is luminously harmonious thanks to the all seeing eye of Paul Cézanne. I see new outlines leaving the Chicago painting no such place. In New York the whole supports the parts. In Chicago I see the whole lost and so almost all is lost. It is also significant that the coherence of the New York painting is reinforced by a fixed ego. I find also lost to Vollard R573, *House Near Gardanne*, 1886-90, Indianapolis Museum of Art and R572, *Hamlet in the Countryside Near Gardanne*, 1886-89, Private Collection. Compare these to R575, *Environs of Gardanne*, 1886-90, Private Collection; where things are as they should be. Of Cézanne's three studies of Gardanne, R569, *Gardanne, Horizontal View*, c. 1885, The Barnes Foundation, Philadelphia, R570, *Gardanne, Vertical View*, c. 1886, The Metropolitan Museum of Art, New York and R571, *Gardanne, Afternoon*, c. 1886, The Brooklyn Museum, New York, NY, I see only the Metropolitan Museum's as intact. Outlines in the Brooklyn painting I see as changed while I see the Barnes as heavily repainted. The difference I suspect is between a work circumspectly altered for Vollard, R571, and the heavy hand of Egisto Fabbri, R569. I also judge R551, the well known *Chestnut Trees at Jas de Bouffon*, 1885-86, Minneapolis Institute of Art, to be a loss to Fabbri. Compare this to R522, *Bare Trees at Jas de Bouffon*, 1885-86, National Museum Western Art, Tokyo. The calligraphic wizardry I see in the Tokyo treetops is lost in a jumble of lines in Minneapolis. The New York Museum of Modern Art's Cézanne "icon", R555, *Large Bather*, ca. 1885, appears to me to be extensively retouched, probably at the behest of Vollard. Taking it from the top I find his hair is as Cézanne left it; but, his face to be in disarray, brows, eyes, nose and mouth redrawn and his jaw and chin cut across by heavy prussian blue lines. Similar dark outlines impair the torso, arms, hands, trunks, legs and feet leaving a sequence of disconnected, anatomically absurd parts while the scumbling of the background destroys the relationship between figure and landscape. Compare this bather to its forebear, the central bather of R211, *Bathers at Rest*, 1876-77, the great, *Caillebotte Bathers*, in the Barnes Foundation. The Barnes bather is if anything more radical in appearance, but follow Cézanne's perspective and he becomes a coherent assemblage of forms that fit beautifully into equally unconventional surroundings. Two other bather compositions I suspect lost to Vollard are R553, *Bathers Before a Tent*, 1883-85, Staatsgalerie, Stuttgart and R665, *Bathers*, ca 1890, Musée d'Orsay. As best I can determine these works as seen in a Vollard photograph of the Cézanne room of the 1904 Salon d'Autome were still intact at the time. Vollard would seem to have had them "fixed" after they came back from the show.[64] The multi figure bather composition R666, St. Louis Museum of Art, ca. 1890, is I think another 'lost' Cézanne. But in this case the culprit, on the basis of perspective and ownership, would seem to be Claude Monet.[65] In the early nineties Cézanne painted a group of pictures of men playing cards using as models workers from the Jas de Bouffon estate; R704 through R717. I see R706, the largest of these, *Card Players*, 1890-92, Barnes Foundation, Philadelphia as compromised by Semitic perspective outlines rendering its forms detached and crudely angular. Compare this to R707, *The Card Players*, 1890-92, The Metropolitan Museum of Art, New York; a monumentally coherent Cézanne, Poussin revisited.[66] Cézanne's wife, Hortense, sat many times for him and most of these portraits are intact. One that as I say above is a loss to Fabbri. is Boston's R324. Another I see as changed is R576, 1886-87, Philadelphia Museum of Art. This time the culprit would seem to have been Henri Matisse.[67] Lost I presume to Vollard are R683, *Madame Cézanne, 1888-90*, Barnes Foundation, Philadelphia and R655, *Madame Cézanne in a Yellow Chair*, 1888-90, Metropolitan Museum of Art, New York . In the latter case I think Vollard's agent has left us a cockeyed Hortense with mangled hands and disarranged dress in a room that collapses around her. Around the year 1890 Cézanne painted four much admired studies of a young Italian boy, a model, wearing a red vest: R656, *Boy in a Red Vest*, 1888-90, Barnes Foundation, Philadelphia; R657, *Boy in a Red Vest*, 1888-90, The Museum of Modern Art, New York; R658, *Boy in a Red Vest*, 1888-90, E. G. Bührle Collection, Zurich and R659, *Boy in a Red Vest*, 1888-90, National Gallery of Art, Washington, D.C. Of the four I find that only R657 in the Museum of Modern Art, as an intact Cézanne. I see R656 and R658 as probably Vollard victims, while R659 in the National Gallery appears to me to be an Egisto Fabbri repaint. Rose Conil, Paul's married sister lived in a country house at Bellevue just east of Aix. The house and the surrounding countryside provided Cézanne with motifs in and about the year 1890. Of these Bellevue paintings I see R692, *Pigeon Tower Bellevue*, The Cleveland Museum of Art and R694, *Pigeon Tower Bellevue*, Private Collection as altered probably for Vollard. Two other landscapes associated with Bellevue also appear to me to have Vollard sponsored "corrections", R761, *Red Earth and Big Pine*, 1890-95, Hermitage Museum, St. Petersburg and the equally well know R718, *Road Provence*, 1890-95, National Gallery of Art, London.[68] During his lifetime some of Cézanne's most admired works were his still lives. Nevertheless, I suspect Vollard had several of these "fixed." Most notably: R800, *Basket of Apples*, ca. 1893 The Chicago Art Institute; R804, the *Unfinished Still Life*, 1895-98, The Museum of Modern Art; New York. Semitic perspective outlines in each case I see altering the work. This brings us to the case of two "classic" still lives I believe altered by Edgar Degas: R681, *The Liqueur Bottle*, c.1890, Private Collection, once the property of Mary Cassat and R772, *The Bottle of Peppermint*, 1893-95, National Gallery of Art, Washington, DC. Both I see as been extensively repainted in a style suggesting Degas and as based on the Hellenic perspective used by Degas. On the other hand I find R675, *The Blue Vase*, 1889-90, Musée d'Orsay to be a work entirely by Degas, a "true" Degas.[69]

1895-1906

The final stage of Cézanne's career begins in November 1895 with the Cézanne show at Ambroise Vollard's Paris gallery. At this time Cézanne emerges from obscurity to become a figure in the Paris art world and beyond. Cézanne's style does not change at this time, but it does during the following decade, perhaps in part due to diabetes and diminished eyesight. He begins using larger patches of color which result in some cases in densely painted fragmented, compositions that leave impressionism further behind. Among such paintings are views of the Chateau Noir, its surroundings and Mount Sainte-Victoire seen from near by his new studio just north of Aix at Les Lauves. In these works I find Cézanne recapturing his youthful exuberance which he joins to twenty years working from nature. From these late years I count 29 paintings I see as altered, probably for Vollard, appendix, R805 through R953. In the summer of 1896 Cézanne goes on vacation with his wife and son to Annecy. There he paints water colors and an oil, a view across the lake R805, *The Lake of Annecy*, 1896, Courtauld

Institute Galleries, London. The ragged appearance of this painting I think reflects not Cézanne's lack of interest in the picture-postcard motif, but to awkward Semitic perspective "corrections" applied I think at the behest of Vollard. I see as a most telling example of Vollard's meddling Vollard's own portrait, R811, *Portrait of Ambroise Vollard*, 1899, City of Paris Collection, Petite Palais. Vollard writes that Cézanne labored long and hard on this work and then left it unfinished. I see its present state as not as Cézanne left it.[70] I see many of the outlines as refashioned using Semitic perspective. The *Portrait* remained in Vollard's personal collection until his death in 1923 when it passed to the City of Paris. Its sad transformation tells me that Vollard truly believed Cézanne needed "improving". Another I think major loss probably to Vollard is R821, *Young Man With A Skull*, 1898-1900, Barnes Foundation, Philadelphia. What was poetic I see as now pathetic, its meaning being dependent on form. Also lost probably to Vollard are two studies of skulls, R821, *Three Skulls, 1898–1900*, *Detroit* Institute of Arts and R822, *Pyramid of Skulls*, 1898-1900, Private Collection. Cézanne's final studies of his gardener, Vallier, are intact including R954, 1906, Private Collection. Cézanne found many late motifs in the Arc Valley including the woods and ledges around the Chateau Noir, the abandoned quarry at Bibémus and views from around his studio at Les Lauves.[71] Of the Bibémus paintings I see as compromise by Semitic perspective outlines thanks I believe to Vollard are R797, *Bibémus Quarry*, 1895, Museum Folkwang, Essen; R799, *Red Rock*, 1895, Musée d'Orangerie, Paris and the well known R837, *Mount Sainte Victoire from the Bibémus Quarry*, ca. 1895, Baltimore Museum of Art. The same is true for R763, *The Millstone*, 1892-04, Philadelphia Museum of Art, a motif from the park of the Chateau Noir. Compare this to R764, *Millstone and Cistern*, 1892-04, Barnes Foundation, Philadelphia, an intact study of a similar motif. Frontal perspective corrections, thanks probably to Vollard, have also cost us R906, *Pines and Rocks*, ca. 1897, The Museum of Modern Art, New York, which Rewald tentatively identifies as a motif near the Chateau Noir and R903, *Rocks and Pines*, Barnes Foundation, Philadelphia, a similar motif that Rewald lists as possibly coming from the Vollard Gallery. Compare these to the beautifully realized R775, *Rocks at*

Fontainebleau, ca, 1893, Metropolitan Museum of Art, New York. Among the densely painted intact works from Cézanne's final years are several views of the Chateau Noir including, R940, *Chateau Noir* 1903-04, Museum of Modern Art New York, R941, *Chateau Noir*, 1903-04, Picasso Museum, Paris and R937, *Chateau Noir*, 1900-04, National Gallery of Art, Washington, DC. I see as altered R909, *Rocks Near the Grottoes above the Chateau Noir*, ca. 1904, Musée d'Orsay. In this case I think the culprit is its one time owner, Henri Matisse.[72] Of Cézanne's late views of Mount Sainte-Victoire I find the following to be altered probably for Vollard: R902, *Mount Sainte-Victoire Seen from the Chateau Noir*, ca. 1901, The Edsil and Eleanor Ford House, Grosse Pointe Shores, Michigan; R910, *Mount Sainte-Victoire Seen from Lauves*, 1902-06, Pearlman Foundation, on loan to Princeton University Museum, NJ; R911, *Mount Sainte-Victoire Seen from Les Lauves*, 1902-04, Philadelphia Museum of Art; R914; *Mount Sainte-Victoire*, 1902-04, Private Collection and R915, *Mount Sainte-Victoire*, The Annenberg Collection, Metropolitan Museum of Art, New York. This brings us back to Cézanne's late *Large Bathers*. The London painting, *R855, Large Bathers*, 1904-6, National Gallery, London and the Barnes painting, R856, *Large Bathers*. 1904-6, Barnes Foundation, Philadelphia, I see as altered thanks to Vollard. R857, *Large Bathers*, 1904-06, Philadelphia Museum of Art, is a pristine Cézanne, a wonder. Every form, every brush stroke celebrates Cézanne's individuality while remaining part of a coherent whole seen Cézanne's way.[73]

This analysis of Cézanne paintings in the Rewald catalogue is intended to right some of the wrong done to this great artist and hopefully make the work more available to us. It is my contention that great art is a driving force in the history of art and to a large extent the work of individuals. Cézanne was a great and influential artist and although some have produced works resembling his none has adopted his all important perspective.[74] Cézanne's influence seems to have been more in the way of ideas about individuality and unconventionality. At this time when ideas rather than form seems to rule the history of art if I am right about the changes to Cézanne did these "fixer uppers" by obscuring the real Cézanne help promote this direction? Be that as it may, it is a mistake to confuse a work of art with ideas about it. A work of art is a world governed by the visual ego, a world in itself.

Both Cézanne and Picasso used perspectives based on disconnection. Disconnection acts to fracture a work and can impede an artist, but both Cézanne and Picasso made disconnection a great asset. Cézanne uses it with a wide view to create works that are coherent yet have great visual diversity. Disconnection is vital a part of Picasso's eleventh Perspective.

APPENDIX.

Cézanne paintings in the Rewald Catalogue Raisonné, that I see as altered, or misattributed.

1. Paintings I see as retouched or repainted perhaps at the behest of Ambroise Vollard:

R121, *The Abduction*, Keynes Collection, on loan to Fitzwilliam Museum, Cambridge.

R136, *The Black Clock*, Private Collection.

R149, *Young Girl at Piano*, Hermitage Museum, St. Petersburg.

R201, *The House of Pére Lacroix*, National Gallery of Art, Washington, DC.

R280, *Village on the Water*, Barnes Foundation, Philadelphia.

R291, *Afternoon in Naples*, Australian National Gallery, Canberra.

R393, *The Seine at Bercy after Guillaumin*, Hamburg Kunsthalle.

R299, *The Eternal Feminine*, J. Paul Getty Museum, Malibu, CA.

R305, *Fruits et Boite a Poudre*, Private Collection.

R407, *Poplars*, Musée d'Orsay, Paris.

R420, *Comptoir, Pommes et Miche de Pain*, Private Collection

R428, *Milk Can and Lemon*, Cincinnati Museum of Art.

R452, *Standing Bather from the Back*, Private Collection.

R464, *Son of the Artist*, Private Collection.

R513, *Plain, Provence*, on loan to the Sammlung Villa Flora, Winterthur.

R516, *L'Estaque, the Morning*, The Israel Museum, Jerusalem.

R525, *The Gardener*, Barnes Foundation, Philadelphia.

R530, *L'Estaque, Rocks, Pines and Sea*, Staatliche Kunsthalle, Karlsruhe.

R533, Sketch for Portrait, Private Collection

R553, *Bathers Before a Tent*, Staatsgalerie, Stuttgart.

R555, *Large Bather*, Museum of Modern Art, New York.

R563, *Peaches and Pears*, Private Collection.

R571, *Gardanne, Afternoon*, Brooklyn Museum, New York.

R572, *House in the Countryside Near Gardanne*, National Gallery of Art, Washington, DC.

R573, *House Before Mount Sainte-Victoire*, Indianapolis Museum of Art.

R619, *Harlequin,* Private Collection.

R626, *The Golf of Marseilles Seen from L'Estaque*, Art Institute, Chicago.

R627, *In the Forest of Fontainebleau*, Private Collection.

R629, *House and Trees*, Barnes Foundation, Philadelphia.

R632, *Hunter's Cabin Provence*, Barnes Foundation, Philadelphia.

R634, *Still life Before a Chest of Drawers*, Fogg Art Museum, Harvard University, Cambridge, MA.

R654, *Curtain*, Abegg Stiflung, Riggisberg.

R655, *Madame Cézanne in a Yellow Armchair*, Metropolitan Museum of Art, New York.

R656, *Boy in a Red Vest*, Barnes Foundation, Philadelphia.

R658, *Boy in a Red Vest*, Sammlung E. D. Bührle, Zurich.

R665, *Bathers*, Musée d'Orsay, Paris.

R677, *Still Life*, Private Collection.

R682, *Reclining Boy*, UCLA, Armand Hamer Museum of Art and Cultural Center.

R683, *Portrait of Madame Cézanne*, Barnes Foundation, Philadelphia

R687, *Alle, Jas de Bouffan*, Private Collection.

R692, *Pigeon Tower, Bellevue*, The Cleveland Museum of Art.

R694, *Pigeon Tower, Bellevue*, Private Collection.

R695, *The Aqueduct*, Pushkin Museum, Moscow

R702, *Terra-cotta Pots and Flowers*, Barnes Foundation, Philadelphia.

R705, *Man With a Pipe*, Private Collection.

R706, *Card Players*, Barnes Foundation, Philadelphia.

R711, *Man with a Pipe*, National Gallery of Art, Washington, DC.

R726, *Reflections in Water*, Private Collection.

R747, *Bathers*, Private Collection.

R760, *The Cracked House*, Metropolitan Museum of Art, New York.

R761, *Large Pine and Red Earth*, currently at the Hermitage Museum, St. Petersburg.

R763, *The Millstone*, Philadelphia Museum of Art.

R767, *Mount Sainte-Victoire*, Barnes Foundation, Philadelphia.

R781, *Woman with a Coffee Pot*, Musée d'Orsay, Paris.

R782, *Still Life with Plaster Eros*, Nationalmuseum, Stockholm.

R797, *The Quarry at Bibémus*, Museum Folkwang, Essen.

R799, *The Red Rock*, Musée du Orangerie, Paris.

R800, *Basket of Apples*, Art Institute, Chicago.

R804, *Still Life*, Museum of Modern Art, New York.

R805, *The Lake of Annecy*, Courtauld Institute Galleries, London.

R806 *Portrait of a Girl with a Doll*, Beggruen Collection, Berlin.

R807, *Portrait of a Young Girl*, whereabouts unknown.

R811, *Portrait of Ambroise Vollard*, Musée de la Ville de Paris, Petite Palais.

R821, *Three Skulls*, Detroit Institute of Arts.

R822, *Pyramid of Skulls*, Private Collection.

R825, *Young Man with Skull*, Barnes Foundation, Philadelphia.

R830, The *Roofs*, Private Collection.

R832, *Church at Montigny-sur-Loing*, Barnes Foundation, Philadelphia

R837, *Mount Sainte-Victoire Seen from Bibémus*, Baltimore Museum of Art.

R841, *Plate of Peaches*, Private Collection.

R855, *Large Bathers*, National Gallery, London.

R856, *Large Bathers*, Barnes Foundation, Philadelphia.

R858, *Bathers*, Private Collection.

R861, *Bathers*, Baltimore Museum of Art.

R877, *Bathers*, Private Collection.

R899, *Mount Sainte-Victoire*, Hermitage Museum, St. Petersburg.

R902, *Mount Sainte-Victoire*, Ford House, Grosse Pointe Shores, MI.

R906, *Pines and Rocks*, Museum of Modern Art, New York.

R910, *Mount Sainte-Victoire*, Private Collection.
R911, *Mount Sainte-Victoire*, on loan to the Philadelphia Museum of Art.
R912, *Mount Sainte-Victoire*, Private Collection.
R915, *Mount Sainte-Victoire*, Private Collection and Metropolitan Museum of Art, New York.
R930, *Turning Road*, National Gallery of Art, Washington, DC.
2. Paintings listed in the Rewald catalogue as possibly be from the Vollard gallery and I suspect retouched or repainted at the behest of Vollard:
R718, *Road in Provence*, National Gallery, London.
R903, *Rocks and Trees*, Barnes Foundation, Philadelphia.
3. Paintings that I believe repainted by Edgar Degas.
R346, *Seven Apples*, Keynes Collection on load to the Fitzwilliam Museum, Cambridge.
R369, *Bather with Raised Arms*, Private Collection.
R416, *Portrait of Cézanne*, Private Collection.
R557, *Two Fruits*, Private Collection.
R681, *The Liqueur Bottle*, Private Collection.
R772, *The Peppermint Bottle*, National Gallery of Art, Washington DC.
4. Paintings from the Rewald Catalogue I think repainted by Camile Pissaro:
R302, *Still Life with Soup Pot*, Musée d'Orsay, Paris.
R313, *Two Vases of Flowers*, Private Collection.
R385, *Portrait of Cézanne*, Musée d'Orsay.
R455, *Struggle of Love, I*, Private Collection.
R577, *Portrait of Jules Peyron*, Private Collection.

5. Paintings repainted I believe by Claude Monet:
R120, *The Negro Scipion*, Museu de Arte de São Paulo assis Chateaubriand.
R666, *Bathers*, Saint Louis Art Museum.
6. Paintings repainted, I believe by Egisto Fabbri:
R124, *Satyrs and Nymphs*, Private Collection.
R324, *Madame Cézanne in a Striped Skirt*, Museum of Fine Arts, Boston.
R341, *Apricots and Cherries*, Private Collection.

R425, *Bowl and Milk Can*, Bridgestone Museum of Art, Tokyo.

R429, *Milk Can and Lemon, II.* Private Collection.

R438, *House in Provence*, National Gallery of Art, Washington DC.

R551, *Chestnut Trees in Winter*, Minneapolis Institute of Arts.

R569, *Horizontal Gardanne*, Barnes Foundation, Philadelphia

R624, *House by the Marne*, Private Collection.

R659, *Boy in a Red Vest*, National Gallery of Art, Washington, DC.

R717, *Bellevue Landscape*, The Phillips Collection, Washington, DC.

R724, *Reflections in Water*, National Gallery of Art, Washington, DC.

7. Paintings repainted, I believe by Emile Schuffenecker:

R444, *The Bay at L'Estaque*, Philadelphia Museum of Art.

R537, *Large Pine. Private Collection.*

8. Paintings I believe repainted by Henri Matisse:

R360, *Three Bathers*, Musée de la Ville de Paris, Petit Palais.

R576, *Portrait of Madame Cézanne*, Philadelphia Museum of Art.

R647, *Fruits and Leaves*, Private Collection.

R909, *Rocks and Grottos*, Musée d'Orsay. Paris.

9. Paintings I believe repainted by Pablo Picasso:

R365, *Five Bathers*, Picasso Museum, Paris.

R395, *The Sea at l'Estaque Seen Through Trees*, Picasso Museum, Paris.

10. Paintings in the Rewald Catalogue I believe on t misattributed .
R8, R13, R21, R43, R47, R71, R73, R84, R88, R96, R110, R129, R131, R143, R159, R170, R172, R173, R179, R182, R188, R195, R199, R205, R206, R207, R208, R209, R210, R2ll, R212, R213, R221, R223, R225, R227, R231, R232, R233, R336, R241, R255, R265, R266, R274, R277, R298, R304, R306, R312, R315, R317, R318, R319, R322, R327, R330, R335, R336, R347, R352, R353, R355, R356, R357, R358, R411, R412, R424, R446, R448, R469, R473, R480, R489, R493, R494, R498, R499, R548, R597, R616, R710, R733, R737, R750, R752, R675, R802, R820, R850, R866, R934, R935, R936, R944 and R948.

PICASSO NOTES

1. I know of no previous explanations of the works of Picasso and Cézanne consistent with these presented here including my own, Peter Moak, *Seeing Picasso*, 2006, Trafford Publishing, Victoria, Canada.

2. The visual ego described here differs from that of Ernest Mach who decsribes what he calls the phenomenal ego which James J. Gibson calls the visual ego. In both cases the ego is a visual world as seen from one eye that includes parts of the viewer. I describe the visual ego as an imagined presence, a self, in relation to which we see the visual world. See James J. Gibson *The Perception of the Visual World*, 1950, 27 and 225.

3. The explanation of Picasso's works has evolved in stages over the years. Daniel-Henry Kahnweiler calls the cubism of Picasso and Braquel, a rational combination of abstract forms and real details. Kahnweiler's does not refer to specific works and is not consistent. Picasso's works. Daniel-Henry Kahnweiler's *The Rise of Cubism*, first published 1920. A second stage is exemplified by Alfred Barr's *Picasso: Fifty Years of His Art,* 1946. Barr supports Kahnweiler's idea of a method and then contradicts this by describing works as disintegrated images. By this time Picasso's work is largely

explained by reference to other works. of art . A third stage begins with Robert Rosenblume's *Cubism and Twentieth Century Art*, 1960 and is epitomized in Leo Steinberg's "What About Cubism" in *Picasso in Perspective*, 1975, G. Schiff ed. These writers reject the idea of a method and see the works as deliberately ambiguous and contradictory and explain them with an ever widening sphere of influences. The fourth stage which prevails today accepts the works as ambiguous and contradictory and interprets them in the the context of cultural, biographical, political, historical, philosophic and or linguistic influences depending on the author. For a biographical approach see Mary Martha Gedo, *Art as Autobiography*, 1980. For a political explanation see Patricia Leighton, *Re-Ordering the Universe: Picasso and Anarchism*. 1897-1914, 1989. For a feminist reading see Anna C. Chave "New Encounters with *Les Demoiselles d'Avignon*, Gender, Race and the Origins of Cubism," The *Art Bulletin*, 76, no. 4. 1964, 596. Other studies of Picasso's "cubism" include: Christine Poggi, *In Defiance of Painting; Cubism, Futurism and the Invention of Collage*, 1992; T. J. Clark, *Farewell to an Idea: Episodes from a History of Modernism*, 1999, Chapter 4, "Cubism and Collectivity",169; Pepe Karmel, *Picasso and the Invention of Cubism*, 2003 and Lisa Forman in a review of four books concerning Picasso: Elizabeth Cowling, *Picasso Style and Meaning*, 2002; Pepe Karmel (as above); Natasha Staller, *A Sum of Distructions, Picasso's Cultures and the Creation of Cubism, 2001* and Jeffrey Weis, Valerie Fletcher and Kathryn Tuma, *The Cubist Portraits of Fernande Olivier*, exh. cat. 2003, National Gallery of Art, Washington D.C., *Art Bulletin*, 2004, Vol. LXXXVI, no. 3, 614. I find none of the above descriptions and explanations to be correct. I find semiology a linguistic approach to be particularly ineffective. See Rosalind Krauss, "The Motivation of the Sign" and Yve-Alain Bois, "The Semiology of Cubism" 169-208, both in Lynn Zelevansky and William Rubin, *Picasso and Braque a Symposium*, Museum of Modern Art, 1992, New York City.

4. For a biography of Picasso see John Richardson, *A Life of Picasso*, vol. I-III. 1881-1906, 1991, *A Life of Picasso: The Cubist Rebel*, Vol. II, 1996 and *A Life of Picasso: The Triumphant Years*, Vol. III, 2007. For *Science and Charity* see Vol. I, 8 about

5. I find Picasso to have been dyslexic because of his handwriting but I see that it no way influenced his art.

6. See Pierre Daix, Georges Boudaille with Jean Rousselet, *Picasso: The Blue and Rose Periods*, 1967, 122, no. II 10, on Picasso's *Moulin de la Galette*.

7. See Ron Johnson "Primitivism in the Early Sculpture of Picasso" *Arts Magazine*, Vol. 49, no. 10, 1975, 64, for the influence of Gauguin on Picasso, Picasso's visit to Paco Durio's studio and the drawing *Parisienne with Exotic Figures*.

8. See Bernard Dornival, "Sources of the Art of Gauguin from Java, Egypt and Ancient Greece," *Burlington Magazine*, 93, No 577, 1951, 118 for the influence of Indonesian art on Gauguin. See also M. Maligne, *Letres de Gauguin*, 1946, 157, LXXX for a letter from Gauguin to Emil Bernard on Gauguin's visits to the fair.

9. See C. Frésches-Thory, "*Portrait of a Woman with Still Life by Cézanne*," in *Art of Paul Gauguin*, exh, cat., 1988, National Gallery of Art, Washington D.C. 192, 111, for a discussion of the relationship Gauguin's relationhip to Cézanne.

10. See Daix and Boudaille (as in no. 6) 197, for *Blue Room*.

11. See Daix and Boudaille (as in no. 6) 229. for *The Blind Man's Meal*. See also Elizabeth Cowling and John Golding, *Objects into Sculpture*. exh, catalogue (London, The Tate Gallery,2994) 231 for the sense of touch in *The Blind Man's Meal*.

12. See Daix and Boudaille (as in no. 6) 308, nos. XV 57-61, for drawings for *Peasants and Oxen* based on peripheral perspective including one in a letter to Gertrude Stein, August 17, 1906.

13. See Daix and Boudaille (as in no. 6) 324, no. XV 115, for *Two Nudes*. See Helen Seckel, ed. *Les Demoiselles d'Avignon*,

vol. I, exh. catalogue, Picasso Museum, 1988, Carnet 1, 104 for two drawings related to *Two Nudes*. These drawings based on the Third perspective used by Picasso, numbers 13R, 24R and 26R are oddly compartment as if Picasso was searching for a new way to subdivide images.

14. See Richardson (as in no. 4) vol. I, 403, for the influence of the Cézanne and Matisse portraits on Picasso. See Irene Gordon, ed. *Four Americans in Paris*. exh. cat., Museum of Modern Art, New York City, 1970, 89, for a photograph of these portraits on Gertrude Stein's wall.

15. See Daix and Boudaille (as in no. 6) 321, no XVI 10, for information about the *Portrait of Gertrude Stein*. See also 305, nos. XV 45-47, for three other works by Picasso where only the face has been changed using his third perspective. See James Johnson Sweeny "Picasso and Iberian Sculpture, *The Art Bulletin*, 23, no. 3. 1941, for the 1906 influence of Iberian Sculpture on Picasso. See Robert S Lubar, "Unmasking Pablo's Gertrude: Queer Desire and the Subject of Portraiture", *The Art Bulletin*, 79, no. 1, 1997, 57, where the head of Gertrude Stein is seen as the product of gender instability.

16. See Seckel (as in no.13) Carnet 4, 170, for drawings of the figure with raised rectangular arms, 1R, 1V, 2R, 2V, 3R and 4R and Carnet 6, 186, a six figure Picasso's third perspective composition. Picasso could have seen Attic Geometric Vase painting at the Louvre. See E. Pottier, *Vases Antiques Du Louvre*, 1897, A 541 and Pepe Carmel, (as in no.1) 52 who points out the influence of Attic Geometric Vase painting on Picasso.

17. See Marie-Lowa Besnard-Benadoc, Michélet-Ribet and Hélen Seckel, *The Picasso Museum Paris, Paintings*, 1986, 40, no, 14 for drawing *Nude with Raised Arms from the Back*. See Pierre Daix and Jean Rousselet, *Picasso: Catalogue Raisonné de l'Oeuvre Peint, 1907-1916*, 1997, 194, no.18 for an oil sketch of *Figure from the Back*, based on Picasso Perspective Four One dated May 07 which provides an aproximate

date for the discovery of Picasso Perspective. See Seckel (as in no.13) Carnet 4, 171. 5V. 6V, 7R, 7V, 172, 8R, 8V, 9R, 9V, 10R and 174, 18V for drawings of the figure with rectangular arms based on Picasso Perspective Four.

18. See Seckel (as in no.17) Carnet 5, 182. This catalogue, *Exposition H. Daumier, Gallerie L. et P. Rosenberg Fils*, April 1907 contains three Picasso Perspective Four drawings of this figure. See also Carnet 5, 314 for an infrared photograph of a Picasso Perspective Five painting *Woman with Joined Hands* with underlying sketches based on Picasso Perspective Four. See Bernard-Bernadoc (as in no. 17) 40, no. 14 for this painting. See Michel Richet, The Picasso Museum Paris, *Drawings, Watercolors and Pastels*, (New York, Aarams, 1989) 72, nos. 137, 138 and 139 for drawings of this figure.

19. See G. Burgess, "The Wild Men of Paris" *The Architectural Record*, 27, no. 5, May 1910, 400-14, for a photograph showing this finial on Picasso's wall.

20. See Pierre Daiz "Histoire de *Demoiselles d'Avignon* Revise a l'Aide des Carnets de Picasso" in Seckel (as in no. 15) Carnet 4, 526 for the suggestion that the watercolor *Five Nudes* post dates the first version of *Les Demoiselles d'Avignon*.

21. Andre Malraux, *Les Tete d'Obsidiene*, 1947, 17 on Picasso's visit to the Trocodéro. The exact date of this visit is not known.

22. See Anatoly Podsik, *Picasso the Artist's Work in Soviet Museums*, 1972, 25, showing the Picasso Perspective Five painting *Friendship*, the Hermitage, as dated 1908 indicating that Picasso continued to use Picasso Perspective Five into 1908. Thus *Les Demoiselles d'Avignon* may have been finished using Picasso Perspective Six later in the spring of 1908.

23. On *Landscape Rue des Bois* see Daix and Rousellet (as in no.17) 226.

24. See Pierre Daix, " The Chronology of Cubism: New Data on the Picasso-Braque Dialogue" in Zelevansky (as in no, 1), 311, fig. 7. Reproduced is a photograph of *Three Women*

showing it as a perspective 5 work and on 315, fig. 13 is the painting as a perspective 6 work.

25. See Leo Steinberg "Resisting Cubism," *Art in America*, 66, no. 6, Dec. 1978, 114 and "The Polemical Part," *Art in America*, 67, March-April, 1979, 114. Steinberg sees the women as distorted and sexually ambiguous.

26. See Judith Cousins "Documentary Chronology," in Rubin ed., exh. cat. *Picasso and Braque: Pioneering Cubism*, Museum of Modern Art, New York City, 1989, 348 and Daix (as in no. 24) 306, for the possible date of the Picasso-Braque meeting. See Daix (as in no. 24) 311 for Braque's *Large Nude*.

27. See John Golding, *Cubism: A History and Analysis*, 1968, 134, for the spread of Cubism.

28. See William Rubin, *Picasso in the Collection of The Museum of Modern Art*, 1972, 138 on *The Reservoir*. Picasso's summer 1909 portraits of Fednande are based on perspective 7 The *Portrait of Fernande*, Museum of Modern Art, New York, I find to have been repainted in the fall of 1909 using perspective 8 The plaster Head of Fernande, fall 1909, is based on Picasso perspective 8 The bronze casts after the plaster that was sold to Ambroise Vollard are based on frontal perspective and not on Picasso's Perspectives. See Jeffrey Weis, Valerie Fletcher and Kathryn A. Tuma, exh. catalogue, Picasso, *The Cubist Portraits of Fernande Olivier*, 2003, National Gallery of Art, Washington D.C.

29. See Rubin (as in no. 28) 62, for an explanatory drawing of *Still Life and a Liqueur Bottle*. See Natasha Staller on Picasso and cinema, *Sum of Destructions: Picasso's Cultures and the Creation of Cubism*, (Yale University Press, 2001) 143.

30. See Rubin (as in no. 28) 66 and John Richardson (as in no. 4), Vol. II, 150 for circumstances surrounding the painting of *Girl with a Mandolin* (Fanny Tellier).

31. For a photograph showing the Picasso perspective eight version of *Guitarist* see Daix and Rosselet (as in n.17) 357.

32. See Daix and Rousselet, 1997 (as in no. 17) 259 on the *Kahnweiler portrait*. See John Richardson, *Picasso an*

American Tribute, exh. cat., Saidenberg Gallery, New York City, 1962, no,2 on the *Kahnweiler portrait* and the identification by Picasso of the image of a roof finial in the painting.

33. See André Salmon on the rational nature of African and Oceanic art "Histoire anecdotique du cubisme," in *La Jeune Painture Francaise*, 1912, (Paris, Société de trent,, Albert Messein) 43.

34. See Daix and Rousselet, 1997 (as in no. 17) 259, for the *Boston Woman*.

35. See Daix and Rousselet, 1997 (as in no. 17) 269 for *Landscape by Céret*.

36. See Rubin (as in no. 29) 68, for *Ma Jolie*. See Richet (as in no. 19) for nos. 277, 278 and 296 three studies for *Ma Jolie*. 278 includes likenesses of Eva and Picasso.

37. See Daix and Rousselet, 1977 (as in no. 17) 178 for information on *Still Life with Chair Caning*. See Christine Poggi, *In Defiance of Painting: Cubism, Futurism and the Invention of Collage* (Yale University Press, 1992) for a discussion of the "untransformed" materials in *Still-Life with Chair Caning*.

38. See Daix and Rousselet, 1997 (as in no.17) 123 for *Man with a Guitar*, 357 and for the summer 1912 photograph that shows its perspective 10 sate.

39. See Robert Rosenblum, "Picasso and the Typography of Cubism," in Roland Penrose and John Golding ed. *Picasso in Retrospect*, 1973, 49. In this essay Rosenblum introduces the reading of Picasso's newspaper clippings.

40. See Anne Umland "The Process of Imagining a Guitar," in Anne Umland ed. *Picasso's Guitars: 1912-14*, exh. catalogue, 2011, Museum of Modern Art, New York City, 17, on Picasso's *Guitar*. See William Rubin ed. *Primitivism in Twentieth Century Art*, exh, catalogue, 1984, 20, for influence of the *Grebo Mask* on *Guitar*. The cardboard version is based on Picasso Perspective Twelve while the metal reproduction, 1914, is based on Semitic perspective.

41. See Rubin (as in no.28) 92, on *Pipe, Glass and Bottle of Rum*, March 1914. Picasso dated this work perhaps to mark the change in perspective.

42. See Rubin (as in no,28) 98, on *Harlequin* and where it states that Alfred Barr identified *Harlequin* as the work Picasso refers to in his letter to Gertrude Stein. This letter is in the Archives Collection of American Literature, Beineche Rare Book Library, Yale University.

43. See Kirk Varnedoe, "Picasso's Self Portraits" in William Rubin ed. *Picasso and Portraiture*, exh. cat. Museum of Modern Art, New York City, 1996, 145, and note 43 for the Harlequin held Picasso portrait.

44. I seem to be alone in identifying the image of Eva in this area. See John Richardson *A Life of Picasso*, Vol. II, 1007-1917, 1996, 375 and 386 on the death of Eva Gouel.

45. See Daix and Rousselet, 1997 (as in no.17) 293 on *Nude Woman, "Jaime Eva."*

46. See Daix and Rousselet, 1997 (as in no.17) 295 on *Still Life (au Bon Marché)*. See Robert Rosenblum (as in no. 40) for a lascivious reading of this work. Rosalind Krause in Zelevansky (as in no.1) 81 takes exception with this reading as do I. See Richardson (as in no.4) 278 on Frika.

47. See William Rubin "Reflections on Picasso and Portraiture" in Rubin (as in no.43) 68, for a different view of *Still Life with a Pedestal Table*. See Bernhard Geisen, *Picasso: Painter Graver*, 1955, 219 for Picasso's 1905 dry point, *Salome*. John Richardson describes the Marie Walter image hidden in this still life and makes reference to Picasso's quixotic penchant for anthropomorphic still life. See Richardson (as in no, 4, Vol. III, 440 and 149-150).

48. See Francoise Gilot, *Life with Picasso*, 1946, 219 for the painting of *The Kitchen* version II. It would seem that Francoise did not know of the painting's hidden portraits.

49. See Rubin (as in no. 28) 112 and 114 on *Three Musicians* and *Three Women at the Spring*.

50. See Rubin (as in no, 28) 138, on *Girl Before a Mirror*.

CÉZANNE NOTES

51. See John Rewald, *The Paintings of Paul Cézanne: A Catalogue Raisonné*, (New York: Harry N. Abrams Inc. 1996). Numbers in this text prefixed by R refer to entries in the Rewald catalogue. Dates used are those of the Rewald catalogue unless otherwise noted. The Emile Bernard photograph is in the Vollard archives, Musée d' Orsay, Paris and reproduced p.511, Rewald Catalogue.

52. For Cézanne criticism see Joseph J. Rishel and Francoise Cachin "A Century of Cézanne Criticism" in *Cézanne*, exh. cat. Francoise Cachin, Isabelle Cahn, Walter Feilchenfelt, Henri Layrette and Joseph Rishel (Harry N Abrams Inc., New York, in association with the Philadelphia Museum of Art, 1996) 23-75 and George Heard Hamilton "Cézanne and His Critics" in *Cézanne: The late Work* , exh. cat. William Rubin ed. (The Museum of Modern Art, New York, 1977) 139-147. Cézanne criticism based on Cézanne's supposed "flawed" perspective evolved from being largely negative to largely positive based on various interpretations of the same "flaws". It is hard to find value in criticism or explanations based on works not correctly seen.

53. After 1895 Vollard came to control most of Cézanne's unsold works. See Robert Jensen "Vollard and Cézanne"

in *Cézanne to Picasso: Ambroise Vollard, Patron of the Avant Garde* exh. cat. ed. Rebecca Robinow (Metropolitan Museum of Art, New York, 2006) 28. Jensen questions Vollard's business practices and treatment of artists as has John Rewald. See John Rewald *Cézanne and America, Dealers, Collectors, Artists and Critics 1891-1921* (New York Graphic Society), 47. More specifically there is the case of the Cézanne lithograph, *Large Bathers*, published by Vollard. See Douglas Druick, "Cézanne Lithographs" in *Cézanne: The Late Work*, exh. cat. ed. William Rubin (The Museum of Modern Art, New York, 1977) 119-37. For the color lithograph, *Large Bathers,* see Lionello Venturi, *Cézanne, Son Art--Son Oeuvre.* (Editions Paul Rosenberg, Paris, 1936). Venturi 1157. This print is based on frontal perspective rather than Cézanne perspective making it a copy of rather than a Cézanne. *Small Bathers*, Venturi 1156 and *Portrait of Cézanne*, Venturi 1158 are based on Cézanne perspective. Druick describes Vollard's practice of having his printer Auguste Clot "translate" the work of various artists to produce prints that Druick calls facsimiles a practice that was as an issue at the time.

54. See appendix for list of Cézanne paintings I see on the basis of perspective as altered, or misattributed.

55. Monet for most of his career uses Attic perspective with a fixed ego.

56. The under appreciated Achille Emperaire uses Hellenic perspective.

57. Pissaro used fixed ego frontal perspective .

58. Degas used Hellenic perspective while Renoir uses fixed ego Hellenic perspective.

59. Dr. Paul Gachet who opened his studio in Auvers to Cézanne in the seventies was an amateur painter as was his son. On the Gachets see Wlater Feilchenfelt, " On Authenticity" in Rewald, (as in no. 51) vol. I. 13.

60. For Egisto Fabbri see Rewald, *The Paintings of Paul Cézanne,* (as in no. 51) vol I, 230. See R448, *Bathers,* as a copy of a work by Cézanne that is reproduced on page 303.

61. *Three Bathers,* R360, is based on a perspective Matisse introduced in 1907, a wide view fixed ego Hellenic perspective with forms then seen related to the not aligned ego. Unlike Cézanne Matisse leaves forms related to a not aligned ego. *Three Bathers* appears intact in a Vollard photograph of the Cézanne room at the 1904 Salon d'Automne to which it had been lent by Matisse. This photograph is reproduced in Rishel, (as in no.51) 564-65. Matisse's changing of *Three Bathers* and other Cézannes in his possession demonstrates his lack in understanding Cézanne.

62. The perspective used to repaint R365 and R395 is the Seventh Variation of Picasso's Perspective.

63. For these photographs see Rishel, (as in no.1) 564-65.

64. See note 55.

65. See *Cézanne's Card Players,* exh. cat. ed. Nancy Iverson and Barnabay Wright, (The Courtald Gallery in Association with Paul Holbrt Publishing, London, 2011) for Cézanne's card player paintings.

66. I believe Matisse repainted this work on the basis of his ownership and the perspective he used. See note 61.

67. Rewald lists R718 as possibly passing through Vollard's hands. Its altered state makes me believe that it did.

68. Degas it seems had extensive dealings with Vollard. The perspective used in repainting these still lives is wide view Hellenic perspective. R675 is not identified in the Rewald catalogue as coming from the Vollard Gallery. It appears intact in the photographs of the Cézanne room at the 1904 Salon d'Autome Its original owner is listed as Eugene Blot. See note 58. I believe that four other Cézannes based on Hellenic perspective to be misattributed. These are R850, *Man with Crossed Arms,* Private Collection, which appears based on the intact R851, *Man with Crossed Arms, The* Guggenheim Museum, New York, ca.1899, the so called

Clock Maker, R936, *Still Life with White Pitcher*, National Museum of Wales, Cardiff, which appears to be loosely based on R848, *Still Life*, Private Collection; R944, *Woman in Blue, 1902-04, Hermitage Museum*, which appears to be loosely based on R945, *Woman with A Book*, 1902-4, The Phillips Collection, Washington, DC and R948, *The Sailor*, 1902-06, Private Collection, which appears to be a copy of R949, *The Sailor*, The National Gallery of Art, Washington DC. I suspect all four of theses works to be by Edgar Degas because of the wide view Hellenic perspective used and passages that strongly suggest the style of Degas. All four were were sold by Vollard as Cézannes. Did he commission then?

69. See Ambroise Vollard, *Paul Cézanne,*(Paris, 1914) 91-107.

70. Bibémus was a source of the yellow stone with which 17th century Aix was built. As far as I can tell Cézanne painted no views of his beautiful home town. It seems to me that Cézanne was more interested in meaning as generated by form than by the subject.

71. See note 61 above on Matisse's perspectives.

72. Both the Barnes and the London *Large Bathers* show signs of at one time being larger in size. With the Barnes painting there are strips along the right side and at the bottom that appear discontinuous with adjacent surfaces. With the London painting these strips exist at the top and bottom and along the right side. I see these strips preserving the original Cézanne perspective which was not changed when the these works were repainted I believe at the behest of Vollard because they were not visible at that time. The changes in size may have occurred after the paintings were moved from Cézanne's Paris studio to his new studio outside Aix at Les Lauves. See Richard Shiff's review of the Rewald catalogue in *The Art Bulletin*, June 1996, Vol. LXXX, No. 2, 384. Shiff describes these discontinuous strips and suggest that these paintings could have been altered by " an honest admirer or a dishonest entrepreneur." Shiff

also raises the possibility that Vollard had work done on the Barnes bathers with which I heartily agree. John Rewald, *Rewald Catalogue*, 510, also discusses changes to the Barnes and London paintings. Rewald writes that the Barnes *Bathers* was changed by Cézanne after the 1904 photograph was taken. On the changes by Cézanne to the Barnes *Large Bathers* see also T. J. Clark, *Farewell to an Idea, Episodes from a History of Modernism*, 1999, Yale University Press, New Haven, CT, 147. I feel certain that the changes made by Cézanne are not the frontal perspective changes that make the Barnes *Large Bathers* no longer a true Cézanne.

73. See Fred Leeman "Painting 'after' Cézanne" in *Cézanne and the Dawn of Modern Art*, exh. cat. ed. Felix A Bauman, Water Feilchenfeldt, Hubertus Gasser (Hatje Cantz Verlag, Essen, 2004) 170-180. Leeman calls the next generation's response to Cézanne "creative misunderstanding". On Cézanne's influence see also *Cézanne and Beyond*, exh. cat. Joseph J. Rishel and Katherine Sachs (Philadelphia Museum of Art in Association with Yale University Press, New Haven and London, 2009). The two artists who's perspectives come closest to Cézanne's are Henri Matisse and Pablo Picasso. A perspective used by Matisse beginning in 1904-05 is based on a wide view followed by forms rleated to the not aligned ego. This differs from Cézanne perspective in which forms are finally presentsed in relation to the large static aligned ego.

SYNOPSIS

The works of Pablo Picasso and Paul Cézanne are based on particular ways of seeing, perspectives. To understand these perspectives I begin with vision. I then go on to explain the eleven different perspectives Picasso uses during his lifetime by looking at his works. In my second essay I explain Cézanne's perspective. Along the way I identify over ninety or so works by Cézanne that have been altered. In addition to Picasso's dealer Ambroise Vollard I suspect seven others, all artists, altering Cézanne paintings in their possession. They are: Camille Pissaro, four; Edgar Degas, six; Claude Monet, two; Emile Schuffenecker, two; Egisto Fabbri, twelve; Henri Matisse, four and Pablo Picasso two. My goal in all this is to make the works of these great artists available.

BIOGRAPHY

I have been aa art historian for over sixty years. I received a Masters degree from New York University 's Institute of Fine art and a Phd. from the University of Pennsylvania. I taught art history at Villanova University and The University of New Hampshire, but most of my life has been devoted to an effort to understand the visual order that underlies a work of art. In addition to research in libraries I traveled extensively here and in Europe to see works first hand. Now that my traveling days are over due to age and my health I am concentrating of on writing about what I have learned.

www.ingramcontent.com/pod-product-compliance
Lightning Source LLC
Chambersburg PA
CBHW030830060726
47590CB00004B/1482